# Growing *in* Spiritual Maturity

# Growing in Spiritual Maturity

## AN 8-SESSION BIBLE STUDY ON BECOMING MORE GROUNDED IN YOUR FAITH

## JOYCE MEYER

NEW YORK • NASHVILLE

Copyright © 2026 by Joyce Meyer

Cover copyright © 2026 by Hachette Book Group, Inc.

Hachette Book Group supports the right to free expression and the value of copyright. The purpose of copyright is to encourage writers and artists to produce the creative works that enrich our culture.

The scanning, uploading, and distribution of this book without permission is a theft of the author's intellectual property. If you would like permission to use material from the book (other than for review purposes), please contact permissions@hbgusa.com. Thank you for your support of the author's rights.

FaithWords
Hachette Book Group
1290 Avenue of the Americas, New York, NY 10104
faithwords.com
@FaithWords / @FaithWordsBooks

First Edition: April 2026

FaithWords is a division of Hachette Book Group, Inc. The FaithWords name and logo are registered trademarks of Hachette Book Group, Inc.

The publisher is not responsible for websites (or their content) that are not owned by the publisher.

The Hachette Speakers Bureau provides a wide range of authors for speaking events. To find out more, go to hachettespeakersbureau.com or email HachetteSpeakers@hbgusa.com.

FaithWords books may be purchased in bulk for business, educational, or promotional use. For information, please contact your local bookseller or the Hachette Book Group Special Markets Department at special.markets@hbgusa.com.

Library of Congress Cataloging-in-Publication Data has been applied for.

ISBNs: 978-1-5460-0965-8 (trade paperback), 978-1-5460-1059-3 (ebook)

Printed in the United States of America

LSC-C

Printing 1, 2026

# CONTENTS

| | |
|---|---|
| *Introduction* | vii |
| *Before You Start* | ix |

| | |
|---|---|
| Lesson 1: Growing Steadily in Christ | 1 |
| Lesson 2: Renewing Your Mind, Transforming Your Life | 9 |
| Lesson 3: Shining Your Light in a Dark World | 15 |
| Lesson 4: The Power of Prayer That Changes Things | 21 |
| Lesson 5: Letting God's Word Fill Your Life | 27 |
| Lesson 6: Anchored in God's Truth | 33 |
| Lesson 7: Pressing on Toward the Goal | 39 |
| Lesson 8: Knowing Jesus on a Deeper Level | 47 |

| | |
|---|---|
| *Looking Back* | 55 |

# INTRODUCTION

If you desire to become all God wants you to be, you're in the right place. God's promise for us isn't salvation alone—it's a life gradually transformed to reflect His character and love.

When I became a Christian, I loved God, went to church, and knew the basic doctrines of the faith, but I didn't know how to deal with the everyday struggles in my life—or realize that I could live victoriously. Because of that, I wasn't really helping anyone else, and I wasn't happy, either. Then I learned that one of our primary goals as Christians should be to grow in spiritual maturity and become more like Christ. God had so much more for me than I was aware of, and He desires the same for you.

Romans 8:29 says, "For those whom He foreknew [of whom He was aware and loved beforehand], He also destined from the beginning [foreordaining them] to be molded into the image of His Son [and share inwardly His likeness]" (AMPC). That means God's plan is not just for us to believe in Jesus so we can go to heaven, but to allow Him to shape our character to look more like His while we're here on earth.

Spiritual maturity is a process of learning to live like Jesus. It requires knowing God's Word and, with God's help, aligning our lives with it. Growth like this doesn't happen overnight. Philippians 1:6 reminds us, "He who began a good work in you will carry it on to completion until the day of Christ Jesus." He changes us little by little, step-by-step. My hope is that the principles in this study will inspire your spiritual growth, deepen your relationship with Christ, and help you become firmly rooted in the Word. Get ready—your journey has already begun!

# BEFORE YOU START

The Bible is more than a book about theology or a story about eternal life when we die. It also offers us the wisdom we need to live victorious, peace-filled, joyful lives on Earth. Jesus says in John 10:10, "The thief comes only in order to steal and kill and destroy. I came that they may have and enjoy life, and have it in abundance [to the full, till it overflows]" (AMP). This verse isn't just about enjoying life when we go on vacation or when something delightful happens. John 10:10 is talking about the fact that God offers us the ability to find joy in ordinary, everyday life. If the only time we can enjoy ourselves is when something exciting happens, we will miss out on the abundant life Jesus died to give us. But if we learn to live according to God's Word, which requires study and obedience, we can savor each day.

Any time we spend in Scripture is good for us. But we need to do more than simply read God's Word; we need to study it deeply. We may read only one verse or passage for several days, but if we are really examining it and digging in to understand what it means for our lives, that's when it begins to transform us. The Bible teaches and empowers us in amazing ways, but we can discover those truths only when we diligently study it.

This abundant life we're invited to live is only possible because of what Jesus has already done for us. He sacrificed Himself on the cross, bearing the burden and punishment for our sins. As promised, He rose from the dead on the third day and is now seated at the right hand of God. On

Pentecost, another promise was fulfilled, and our heavenly Father sent the Holy Spirit to be in us and with us at all times (Acts 2:1–33)—to teach us, help us, comfort us, and guide and lead us in all things.

Most of the New Testament letters, called the Epistles, were written to young churches and believers who needed to grow in their faith and learn to live God's way. The writers—including the apostles Paul, James, Peter, and John—were trying to help new believers become established in their relationship with God and learn how to live godly lives. That's why the Epistles contain not only valuable theological principles but also important practical advice for our everyday lives. I am excited to know that I will one day go to heaven, but I also want to enjoy the life God has given me today and every day until I get there.

I encourage you to take your time going through this study. Don't just read—pause to reflect. Stop at places that speak to you. Ask how they apply to your life and whether there are any changes you need to make to walk more fully in God's will.

I invite you to answer the questions included throughout this study—they're designed to help you recognize areas where you need to grow. In each lesson, you'll also find a short reading from one of my books, and I've included the titles in case you would like to explore the topics further.

I also want to suggest that you take the time to look up the Scripture references that appear throughout the study. Space does not permit us to print out each verse in full, but you can open your Bible to the references mentioned and read the Scripture passages for yourself. The effort you put into doing this will enhance your overall experience and help you truly absorb the truths of God's Word.

Remember that studying is different from simply reading. When we read, we take in information, but when we study, the information becomes revelation to us—it becomes part of us and transforms our lives and behavior in deeper ways than a quick reading does. When we dig deeper into Scripture, we will uncover hidden treasures that not only help us live more fully for God but also continue to set us free—free to enjoy God and the life He has provided for us through Jesus.

LESSON 1

# Growing Steadily in Christ

## Let's Get Started

Think of someone you know who you consider to be very spiritually mature. What are some characteristics that set that person apart?

_____
_____
_____

## Key Scripture Reading

*Brothers and sisters, I could not address you as people who live by the Spirit but as people who are still worldly—mere infants in Christ. I gave you milk, not solid food, for you were not yet ready for it. Indeed, you are still not ready. You are still worldly. For since there is jealousy and quarreling among you, are you not worldly? Are you not acting like mere humans?*

1 Corinthians 3:1–3

## Dig Deeper

What do you think Paul means here when he talks about being an "infant in Christ" rather than behaving maturely?

## Core Truth

A full-grown man was not born as an adult. He began as a baby and grew gradually until he reached maturity. We are the same way as Christians. We begin as spiritual babies. Paul told the Corinthians that he could not feed them the meat of God's Word because although they should have been farther along in their growth, they were still babies in Christ (1 Corinthians 3:2). We might say that the milk of the Word—the messages that are easy for us to digest—are those that teach us what we have from God by His grace, while the meat of the Word refers to messages that teach us what we should do in light of what God has given us and done for us.

We are to leave the baby stage of Christianity—being concerned mainly with getting our needs met—and gradually grow into spiritual perfection (maturity). In that place of maturity, we are not primarily concerned about our own needs but about how we might serve God.

Not one of us has arrived at a place where we no longer need to grow, but we should be able to see that we are growing, changing for the better, and becoming more like Jesus in our behavior. I frequently say, "I am not where I need to be, but thank God, I am not where I used to be." I am growing, and that is what God expects all of us to do.

The things a baby does that may be considered cute as an infant or toddler are no longer cute when the person is thirty or forty years old and still doing the same things. For example, small children may ask questions continually, and their parents may find their inquisitiveness cute—but by the time they are fully grown, the parents no longer want to be questioned about every action they take. By then a relationship of trust should have been built between them. A small child may talk too much, and we think it is just part of growing up, but when an adult talks too much and never knows when to listen, it annoys us.

We expect babies to be babies, children to be children, and teenagers to be teenagers, but we also expect adults to behave maturely. Paul writes to the Corinthians that when he was a child, he talked like a child, thought like a child, and reasoned like a child; but when he grew up, he put aside childish ways (1 Corinthians 13:11). If we expect our natural children to do that, surely God expects us to do the same regarding spiritual maturity.

Paul could tell that the Corinthians lacked spiritual maturity because there was still jealousy and strife among them (1 Corinthians 3:1–3). In other words, their behavior revealed their level of spiritual maturity. It is no different with us. We can easily locate where we are in our walk with God by listening to ourselves and examining how we behave, especially under pressure. Paul encourages us to examine ourselves to see if we are living as we should (2 Corinthians 13:5). I personally think that taking the time to do this on a regular basis is spiritually healthy. It is not to be done so we can feel guilty or condemned when we recognize our faults, but so the Holy Spirit may help us change.

Unless people know who they are in Christ, they cannot do this, because any fault they find in themselves—or that others point out—immediately makes them feel downcast and condemned. However, when we know that God loves us and never rejects us, we are able to receive correction and actually rejoice in it because we want to be everything God desires us to be.

I would venture to say that it is impossible to reach spiritual maturity without ever receiving correction. We cannot get to where we want to be unless we are honest with ourselves about where we are.

Spiritual "children" are easily affected emotionally by the storms of life, but Paul wants us to mature so that we are no longer manipulated or controlled by our circumstances. Our circumstances may change at any time, but God always remains the same. His Word stands firm and will hold us steady in the storms of life if we let it.

Apparently various doctrines came through the church in those days, as they still do today. In Ephesians 4, Paul said the believers would not be deceived by those doctrines or the ones who preached them if they were spiritually mature. People who are mature are sure about what they believe. They are firmly rooted and grounded in God's Word, and nothing and no one can move them from their position. This does not mean that they are never open to learning new things. They are open-minded, but not double-minded.

### Additional Reading

**From *A Leader in the Making***

In Colossians 1:15, Paul tells us that Jesus is "the exact likeness of the unseen God [the visible representation of the invisible]; He is the First-born of all creation" (AMPC). As believers, we are to be transformed into His image and likeness, and we are to follow in His footsteps.

The greatest goal of every believer, and certainly those of us who want to be used by God in positions of leadership, should be to be more like Christ. We should want to handle situations the way Jesus would handle them and treat people the way Jesus would treat them. We should desire to do things the way He would do them. That should be our goal.

Jesus is to be our example. In John 13:15, He said to His disciples, after washing their feet with the humility of a servant, "For I have given you this as an example, so that you should do [in your turn] what I have done to you" (AMPC). Peter also tells us in 1 Peter 2:21: "For even to this were you called [it is inseparable from your vocation]. For Christ also suffered for you, leaving you [His personal] example, so that you should follow in His footsteps" (AMPC).

The vocation—the high calling—of every believer is to be transformed into the image of Jesus Christ. God will continue working with each of us until we reach the point where we act the way Jesus would in every situation, bearing the same kind of fruit of the Spirit that He demonstrated.

## Think About It

What is one way that you have grown spiritually over time? What is one area where you know you still need to grow?

_____
_____
_____

How do you recognize areas of immaturity in your own life? What steps can you take to address those areas with God's help?

_____
_____
_____

## Supporting Scripture

*If any of you lacks wisdom, you should ask God, who gives generously to all without finding fault, and it will be given to you.*

James 1:5

## Put It to Work

Write down a prayer asking God to grow your maturity in a specific aspect of your life, and pray it throughout the upcoming week.

_____
_____
_____
_____

## Your Personal Response

Take a moment to identify what stage of spiritual maturity you're in. If you're still a baby in the faith, remember: We all start there. What matters most is that you're making progress. The devil wants to condemn you, but God wants to grow you. As Romans 8:1 says, "There is now no condemnation for those who are in Christ Jesus."

Remind yourself of this important truth: "I'm not where I need to be, but thank God I'm not where I used to be." Say it out loud. Write it on a sticky note and place it on your mirror.

When a voice of discouragement starts whispering in your ear, speak God's truth right back. He's not finished with you yet—and that's a promise you can count on!

Finally, think back to the spiritually mature person you know. If you are able to, ask them how God has shaped them throughout their life and what spiritual maturity means to them.

_____
_____
_____
_____
_____
_____
_____

**LESSON 2**

# Renewing Your Mind, Transforming Your Life

## Let's Get Started

Have you ever struggled to implement changes in your life or in the way you think? Why do you think these kinds of changes can be so difficult?

___

___

___

___

## Key Scripture Reading

*Regarding your previous way of life, you put off your old self [completely discard your former nature], which is being corrupted through deceitful desires, and be continually renewed in the spirit of your mind [having a fresh, untarnished mental and spiritual attitude], and put on the new self [the regenerated and renewed nature], created in God's image, [godlike] in the righteousness and holiness of the truth [living in a way that expresses to God your gratitude for your salvation].*

Ephesians 4:22–24 AMP

## Dig Deeper

What do you think it means to be "continually renewed in the spirit of your mind," as it says in this verse?

_____
_____
_____
_____

## Core Truth

When we are born again (receive Christ as our Savior), we are given a new nature and a new heart. Although we have been made new, Paul says that we must daily put on the new self. He means we must choose over and over again to do what we know to be right. We are to completely discard our old way of life, because to be a new creature in Christ and continue in our old ways would be tragic.

In verse 22, Paul says we are to put off the old self, or walk away from old ways, and in verse 24, he says we are to put on the new self, which has been recreated in God's image. That sounds simple enough, but in our experience, we often find that we fail. I have found verse 23 to be very helpful, and I call it the bridge scripture between verses 22 and 24.

If we want to put off the old self and put on the new self, we need to continually be renewed in our minds. This happens as we spend time studying God's Word and meditating on His principles. We are to have a fresh mental and spiritual attitude daily. Our thoughts always precede our actions; therefore, we need to think new thoughts in order to behave according to the new self.

It is very important for us to understand these three verses. We are made new in Christ, but the old nature still tries to rule us. We must say no to it as often as needed, and that could be multiple times each day. We don't receive Christ and then find we are never tempted after that. Our Christian journey is a daily walk, and each good decision we make is another step closer to experiencing the good life God has made ready for us.

You need not feel guilty if you are tempted, because temptation comes to all of us. Just ask the Holy Spirit to make you quickly aware of Satan's strategies and say no to him when he tempts you to do what is wrong.

## Additional Reading

**From *The Love Revolution***

If you want to dedicate yourself to God so He can use you to love and help others, I suggest you pray like this: "Lord, I offer You my eyes, ears, mouth, hands, feet, heart, finances, gifts, talents, abilities, time, and energy. Use me to be a blessing everywhere I go today."

Living this way also means intentionally renewing your mind with the Word of God—reading it, meditating on it, and letting it shape your thoughts each day. Doing this gradually replaces self-centered thinking with God-centered thinking and keeps your heart aligned with the good plans He has for your day.

You will never know the joy of living like this unless you actually try it. I call it a "holy habit," and like all habits, it must be practiced to become one. On some days, I still get caught up with myself, but I am quickly reminded when I lose my joy and enthusiasm that once again I have gotten off track.

> I've been trying to live this way for several years, and at times it has been quite a battle. The "self life" is deeply ingrained in every fiber of our being and does not die easily. I have read books about love, gone over and over what the Bible says about it, and prayed about it. I have talked with friends about it, preached about it, and done all I can to keep it foremost in my thinking. There are times when I realize that I've been selfish again, but I don't get upset, because getting upset with myself only keeps me focused on me. When I fail, I ask God to forgive me and start fresh, and I believe that's the best policy. We spend far too much time feeling bad about ourselves because of the mistakes we make—and that is a waste of time. Only God can forgive us, and He is quite willing to do so if we will simply ask Him.

## Think About It

What motivates your choices on an average day? If you answer yourself honestly, would you say you make most of your choices from a place of love or for other reasons?

_____
_____
_____

In what areas are you still acting from old habits or relying on worldly thinking instead of trusting Jesus?

_____
_____
_____

## Supporting Scripture

*Do not conform to the pattern of this world, but be transformed by the renewing of your mind. Then you will be able to test and approve what God's will is—his good, pleasing and perfect will.*

Romans 12:2

## Put It to Work

Identify an area of your life that Jesus has transformed. Take time this week to reflect on that change, thank Him for it, and ask the Holy Spirit to continue strengthening you in that area.

_____

_____

_____

## Your Personal Response

Which habits or thoughts from your "old self" still influence you the most? Writing a list can help you think clearly, so take some time to do that.

Now, think about a time when God helped you live from your "new self" instead. How did it change things? In what ways did you feel different? What outcome happened that wouldn't have if your old self had been in charge?

Remember, the Word of God is your weapon. What scripture can you use the next time your old self tries to take control? Find one, write it down, memorize it, and declare it.

End your reflection time by telling God about a struggle you're facing. Say, "Lord, I can't handle _____, but You can."

# GROWING IN SPIRITUAL MATURITY

# LESSON 3

# Shining Your Light in a Dark World

## Let's Get Started

Have you ever known someone who truly radiated the love of God? How did their life impact you or those around them?

_____
_____
_____
_____

## Key Scripture Reading

*For once you were darkness, but now you are light in the Lord; walk as children of Light [live as those who are native-born to the Light] (for the fruit [the effect, the result] of the Light consists in all goodness and righteousness and truth), trying to learn [by experience] what is pleasing to the Lord [and letting your lifestyles be examples of what is most acceptable to Him—your behavior expressing gratitude to God for your salvation]. Do not participate in the worthless and unproductive deeds of darkness, but instead expose them [by exemplifying personal integrity, moral courage, and godly character]; for it is disgraceful even to mention the things that such people practice in secret. But all things become visible when they are exposed by the light [of God's precepts], for it is light that makes everything visible.*

Ephesians 5:8–13 AMP

## Dig Deeper

What does it mean to you to be a "child of light"?

_____
_____
_____
_____

## Core Truth

In Ephesians 5, Paul reminds the believing Gentiles that although they were once filled with darkness and participated in evil practices like greed and idolatry (v. 5), they are now new creations filled with light and called to walk in the light. Jesus is the light (John 8:12).

The light is full of goodness and the truth of God's Word. When light floods a dark place, things once hidden are exposed. As we walk in the light of God's truth, evil things are exposed and we see things differently from how we did previously. Doing what is right becomes our primary concern, and we should seek to please God in all things. We all make mistakes, and we make them often, but if our heart's attitude is to do right, God works with us and we are gradually changed more and more into the image of Christ (2 Corinthians 3:18).

We can learn by our experience what is pleasing to God and what isn't. We have the Holy Spirit living inside of us, and He reveals sin to us, helping us know what we should and should not do. One way He does this is by making us a little uncomfortable about what we are doing if it is not right. If we persist in wrong behavior, our ability to experience the Lord's peace and joy will decrease. God's Word says we are to follow peace, and if peace is not present, it is wise to reexamine our actions (Colossians 3:15; Hebrews 12:14).

The Holy Spirit is an encourager, and He works to bring hope and healing to wounded souls. We should work with Him, not against Him. When the prophet Isaiah entered the presence of God, he said that he was ruined because he realized he was a man of unclean lips (Isaiah 6:4–5). Then an angel touched his mouth, his sins were forgiven, and God used him mightily (Isaiah 6:6–7).

I love the ministry of the Holy Spirit in my life because it is a safeguard for me. He points out sin in our lives as well as in the lives of others, and that keeps us safe, as long as we listen to Him. The moment the Holy Spirit shows us sin of any kind, we are to turn away from it and choose to live a lifestyle that is pleasing to God. We are to live as children of the light.

## Additional Reading

### From *Approval Addiction*

When people begin studying God's Word and learn how to live in the light—trusting God even when His light reveals what's been hiding in the darkness—their lives change for the better. God knows everything, and He loves you and me anyway, so we can be totally open and honest with the Lord. He hates pretense, so just be honest.

Ask Him to reveal to you anything you may be hiding from or afraid to face—and then buckle your seat belt. You may be in for the ride of your life. It may be a bumpy ride at times, and frightening at others. You may want to say, "Stop the ride and let me off; I can't take any more!" But one thing is for sure: It is a ride that will eventually take you where you want to go, which is to a life that you can enjoy, one that bears good fruit for God.

God has revealed so much to me about myself that I am amazed. We think we know ourselves, when in reality we are often hiding, not only from others, but especially from ourselves. God had to show me many things about myself that were very uncomfortable—things I rejected at first, thinking, "I can't be that way." Over the years of my spiritual development, He showed me I was hard to get along with, controlling, manipulative, fearful, insecure, and hard-hearted. I talked too much. I pretended I didn't need anyone, when in reality I was very needy indeed. I acted as tough as a raging lion on the outside, but on the inside I was as weak as a newborn kitten. I blamed my past for everything I did wrong. I made excuses for bad behavior rather than taking responsibility for it. The list is too long to continue, but the good news is that I can now say, "I used to be that way, and I have changed."

As I always say, "I am not where I need to be, but thank God I am not where I used to be. I am okay, and I am on my way!"

Don't be afraid of your weaknesses any longer. Don't allow them to make you hate yourself. Give them all to God, and He will surprise you by using them. Give Him everything you are and especially everything you are not. When you do surrender to God in this way, you will experience a release from those things that burden you. You will be able to live light and free.

## Think About It

How can you reflect the light of Jesus in your words, actions, or attitude this week?

_____
_____
_____
_____

Think about a time when you took responsibility for something that was your fault. How did you grow from that? Is there anything in your life that you need to take responsibility for now?

_____
_____
_____
_____

## Supporting Scripture

> *Now the Lord is the Spirit, and where the Spirit of the Lord is, there is freedom. And we all, who with unveiled faces contemplate the Lord's glory, are being transformed into his image with ever-increasing glory, which comes from the Lord, who is the Spirit.*
>
> 2 Corinthians 3:17–18

## Put It to Work

Take a moment to reflect. Is there any area of your life the Holy Spirit is gently bringing into the light? Ask Him to show you clearly and to give you the grace and strength to walk in His truth.

## Your Personal Response

Read Matthew 5:14–16. When has God used you to bring His light into someone's darkness? Take a moment to reflect on that experience. How did it feel? How did God work through your obedience?

Where, specifically, could you let your light shine this week—at work, with friends, or with family? Choose one specific area where you will intentionally share God's truth and be a source of encouragement this week. Then write down the answers to these three questions:

1. What is the need?
2. What will you do?
3. When will you do it?

Writing it down helps settle it in your mind and often leads to following through on what you've committed to do.

LESSON 4

# The Power of Prayer That Changes Things

## Let's Get Started

How have you experienced the power of prayer—either personally or in the life of someone you care about?

_____
_____
_____
_____

## Key Scripture Reading

*For this reason, since the day we heard about you, we have not stopped praying for you. We continually ask God to fill you with the knowledge of his will through all the wisdom and understanding that the Spirit gives, so that you may live a life worthy of the Lord and please him in every way: bearing fruit in every good work, growing in the knowledge of God, being strengthened with all power according to his glorious might so that you may have great endurance and patience, and giving joyful thanks to the Father, who has qualified you to share in the inheritance of his holy people in the kingdom of light.*

Colossians 1:9–12

## Dig Deeper

With this passage in mind, why do you think it's important to know God's will for your life?

_____
_____
_____
_____

## Core Truth

Paul wanted the early Christians to go deeper in their faith. The Amplified Bible renders the last part of Colossians 1:10 this way: "bearing fruit in every good work and steadily growing in the knowledge of God [with deeper faith, clearer insight and fervent love for His precepts]." The way to go deeper is to steadily grow in your personal knowledge of God. I don't mean only knowledge about God, but personal experience of His faithfulness and love for you. This will strengthen your faith, increase your spiritual insight, and cause your love for Him to become more fervent.

One way we grow in our relationship with God is to mature in prayer. What if we were to pray each morning, "God, I want to please You today. Help me walk in Your will and be a blessing to others"? But we usually approach God with a list of things we want Him to do for us. "God, You've got to change my spouse. God, I need that promotion at work. God, I need a bigger house"—and on and on. But as we grow spiritually, our prayers change. Studying the prayers of Jesus and the prayers of Paul helped me see how self-centered my prayers were, and I felt God challenge me not to ask for one more "thing" until He released me to do so. It was like fasting from selfish, carnal prayers.

For six months, I did not feel I could ask God for anything materialistic. All I could say was "God, I need more of You." Of course, various requests would come to mind and sometimes come out of my mouth. When they did, I simply said, "Never mind, God. I just need more of You."

The reason asking for more of God is so important is that everything we need is found in Him. We are complete in Him (Colossians 2:10). In Him, we have everything we need to live a godly life (2 Peter 1:3). Our peace is in Him, our joy is in Him, and our strength is in Him.

This does not mean we do not or cannot desire other things, whether they are offered by the world or meet our practical needs. But God wants us to keep Him first, to hunger for Him above all else, and to be completely satisfied with Him. God was teaching me this lesson, and it was an important one that marked a good change in my walk with Him. If we put Him first, He will add all the other things we need (Matthew 6:33).

## Additional Reading

**From *In Pursuit of Peace***

There is nothing we can give to God except ourselves. Through prayer, we offer our hearts, show appreciation for all He has done for us, and praise Him for His goodness.

Trust yourself to God—He wants you! He wants to take care of you and be your everything. Total surrender of your life in prayer brings an awesome peace with God—the peace that surpasses understanding.

We maintain this peace when we surrender our guilt for past sins to Him. God wants us to ask for and receive His free gift of forgiveness, which has always been available to us. I encourage you to make it a habit: When you ask God to forgive your sins, follow up by saying, "I receive that forgiveness right now, and I let go of the guilt."

Learn to receive. Picture yourself as a branch hanging onto the Vine, receiving life from Him. Pray, "I receive, Lord. I give myself to You, and I receive You as my everything in life: my Savior, Lord, Strength, Peace, Righteousness, Joy, Justification, Sanctification, and all other blessings."

All the branch can do is receive what the Vine offers. To receive means to act like a receptacle and simply take in what is being offered. Live as a receiver by grace, not by works or your own effort.

Living by grace is trusting in God's ability instead of relying on our own work to accomplish what needs to be done. And look what Christ can do: Hebrews 1:3 says that He upholds and maintains and guides and propels the universe by "His mighty word of power" (AMPC)!

God makes this earth and all of the planets and stars spin perfectly through space. We don't even know how big the universe is. If He can do that, shouldn't we relax, knowing He can take care of us, too? If He can run the entire universe, surely He can guide and sustain each of us when we come to Him in prayer.

## Think About It

What do you find easiest to pray for? What do you find hardest to pray for?
_____
_____
_____
_____

How have you experienced God's faithfulness in your life? How does reflecting on this affect your prayers?

_____
_____
_____

## Supporting Scripture

*But seek first his kingdom and his righteousness, and all these things will be given to you as well.*

Matthew 6:33

## Put It to Work

Write a prayer asking God to help you know Him better and experience His presence more fully, and make it a point to pray this prayer throughout the week.

_____
_____
_____

## Your Personal Response

Open your Bible and read Colossians 1:9–12 slowly. Don't rush through it. Really let it sink in. Here's the passage from the Amplified Bible:

> For this reason, since the day we heard about it, we have not stopped praying for you, asking [specifically] that you may be filled with the knowledge of His will in all spiritual wisdom [with insight

into His purposes], and in understanding [of spiritual things], so that you will walk in a manner worthy of the Lord [displaying admirable character, moral courage, and personal integrity], to [fully] please Him in all things, bearing fruit in every good work and steadily growing in the knowledge of God [with deeper faith, clearer insight, and fervent love for His precepts]; [we pray that you may be] strengthened and invigorated with all power, according to His glorious might, to attain every kind of endurance and patience with joy; giving thanks to the Father, who has qualified us to share in the inheritance of the saints (God's people) in the Light.

What jumps out to you about Paul's way of praying? Read the passage again, and circle or underline the words that speak to your heart.

Now, finish this sentence: "If I prayed more like Paul, my prayer life would be different because…"

Take a few quiet moments in prayer, and use some of the words and phrases you underlined, speaking them aloud as you ask God to deepen your prayer life and strengthen your faith in Him.

_____
_____
_____
_____
_____
_____
_____
_____

LESSON 5

# Letting God's Word Fill Your Life

## Let's Get Started

What is a Bible verse you find especially encouraging, comforting, or convicting?

_____
_____
_____

## Key Scripture Reading

*Let the message of Christ dwell among you richly as you teach and admonish one another with all wisdom through psalms, hymns, and songs from the Spirit, singing to God with gratitude in your hearts.*

Colossians 3:16

## Dig Deeper

What does it mean for the message of Christ to "dwell among you richly"? What feelings or images does that evoke for you?

_____
_____
_____

## Core Truth

Today's verse isn't so much about singing to each other as it is about keeping your heart happy, your thoughts disciplined, and your life simple. All of these add to our peace. I'm not very good at singing, but I often find myself humming throughout the day, which Ephesians 5:19 calls "making melody in your heart to the Lord" (NKJV). Making melody in your heart to Him keeps negative emotions and attitudes from taking root, and that's always good.

Colossians 3:16 says to "let the message of Christ dwell among you richly," but some other translations render it as "let the word of Christ dwell in you richly." In other words, let the Word of God fill your thoughts. It's important for us to think about and meditate on what God says.

Let me encourage you to ask yourself how much time you spend each day letting Scripture roll over and over in your mind. You may often hear the instruction to "Meditate on the Word," but hearing that will not help you if you do not actually do it. One of the best ways to become rooted and grounded in the truth of God's Word is to take just one or two verses and, throughout the day, meditate on them and think about what they mean. The only way to experience the full benefit of everything God's Word offers is to meditate on it—just as the only way to get the full benefit of the food you eat is to chew it well.

The verse also talks about admonishing one another. Most people do not like to be admonished or told what they are doing wrong. But here Paul teaches us that when correction is necessary, it should be done with wisdom and by a person in whom God's Word dwells. No one wants to be corrected when they are gossiping, acting dishonestly, or spreading rumors, or when their anger is out of control. Yet in certain situations, and in the right spirit, admonishment helps people grow and mature spiritually.

## Additional Reading

**From *Habits of a Godly Woman***

I have said this many times, but I want to repeat it here: God's Word is very precious. It is worth prioritizing, even if you have to get up thirty minutes earlier than you already do. I can truly say that I love His Word, and that it has changed me and changed my life as nothing else could have ever done. I've also seen it bring miraculous changes to the lives of other people. I could speak for hours about how powerful and how wonderful the Word of God is and never grow tired of talking about it. If I could give only one piece of advice to every person I know, I would say that after being saved, the most important thing anyone can ever do is to study, meditate on, and obey God's Word. There are many ways available for us to take in the Word of God. We can read and study the Bible or books about biblical topics that may help us understand the Scriptures more clearly. We also have teachings available to us through other forms of media, including television, the internet, podcasts, and other sources.

Although on the surface the Bible looks like many other books, it is completely unique in both its essence and its impact. God's words are living words, filled with life and power. The power of God is inherent in His words; they save us, heal us, set us free, lead and guide us, comfort us, correct us, and encourage us. Second Timothy 3:16 says, "All Scripture is God-breathed." We can't say that about any other book on earth. The words of Scripture are not words that come from human intellect or words based on human experience. They are words that impart God's life and truth to us.

## Think About It

How can you let the message of Christ fill your life and keep your heart joyful and your thoughts disciplined?

_____
_____
_____

Have you ever received or offered spiritual admonishment? What lessons did you take away from that experience?

_____
_____
_____

## Supporting Scripture

> *Instead, be filled with the Spirit, speaking to one another with psalms, hymns, and songs from the Spirit. Sing and make music from your heart to the Lord, always giving thanks to God the Father for everything, in the name of our Lord Jesus Christ.*
>
> Ephesians 5:18–20

## Put It to Work

What is one area of your life where you need God's freedom, healing, or guidance—whether it's anger, a physical need, a relationship, or something else? Take a moment to find a verse or two in Scripture on that subject and practice meditating on it through the week.

_____
_____

Letting God's Word Fill Your Life

_____
_____

## Your Personal Response

Let's get practical with this instruction: "Let the message of Christ dwell among you richly" (Colossians 3:16).

Break it down and make it personal. Take each of the following words and write what it means to you:

- **Message:** What is the message of Christ?
- **Christ:** Who is He to you today?
- **Dwell:** How is His message taking root in you?
- **Richly:** How can God's Word fill your life today?

From your reflections, jot down two or three simple ways you can make God's Word more central in your daily life this week. Remember, it's not about perfection—it's about progress!

_____
_____
_____
_____
_____
_____
_____

LESSON 6

# Anchored in God's Truth

## Let's Get Started

Have you ever realized that something you believed conflicted with God's Word? How did you respond?

_____
_____
_____
_____

## Key Scripture Reading

*See to it that no one takes you captive through hollow and deceptive philosophy, which depends on human tradition and the elemental spiritual forces of this world rather than on Christ. For in Christ all the fullness of the Deity lives in bodily form, and in Christ you have been brought to fullness. He is the head over every power and authority.*

Colossians 2:8–10

## Dig Deeper

What does it mean to you that you have been "brought to fullness" in Christ?

## Core Truth

Society today is full of philosophy, and when we hear that someone is a philosopher, it can sound quite impressive. But when I looked up the definition of philosopher, I discovered that a philosopher is simply a thinker. Therefore, we can define philosophy as simply a way of thinking about or viewing things.

The internet has made spreading thoughts, ideas, and information faster and easier than ever. People can publicize their philosophies and gain a following very quickly if their ideas are appealing. There are political philosophies, economic philosophies, religious philosophies, philosophies of relationships (such as how people should relate to each other, what constitutes a family, and how marriages and families should operate), and many other types of philosophies.

People can have the philosophy that lying, cheating, and stealing are acceptable. They can think they should live only for the present and not worry about taking care of their physical bodies or preparing wisely for the future. They can have the philosophy that they should not have to work or earn anything for themselves—that everything should be given to them. Almost anyone can find a philosophy that agrees with the way they think—or they can invent one.

Paul writes that such philosophies—ones not based on the truth of Christ—are dangerous and can even take people captive. To be captive means to lose freedom and become subject to someone else's authority. Jesus wants to be the only authority in our lives, and when we allow Him to be in that rightful place, He gives us freedom.

Any philosophy that goes against God's truth has its roots in the enemy. The enemy is a liar (John 8:44), he is a deceiver (Revelation 12:9), and he constantly tries to get us to believe things that are not true. Sometimes what he gets us to believe is not categorically untrue; there is just enough nonsense mixed in to make it false. The only way we can ever avoid being deceived is to pray regularly that we shall not be deceived and to stay in God's Word, which is full of truth.

A prevalent philosophy today says that there is no firm, exact, or absolute truth and that everything is relative. I cringe inside when I hear that. People who talk about it say that the generation living today is different than previous generations. They declare that we are now living in the twenty-first century and that, in fact, everything is different. Yes, I agree that some things are different, but God's Word has not changed. No matter what century people live in, the Word of God is still the only truth that sets us free (John 8:32), and it is the only thing that will work in our lives. Isaiah prophesied thousands of years ago: "The grass withers and the flowers fall, but the word of our God endures forever" (Isaiah 40:8).

Paul knows that only God's truth can stand against the world's thought systems. He issues a clear warning to his readers, urging them not to let philosophies or ways of thinking take them captive. He refers to these as "hollow and deceptive philosophy" and says that they depend on human beings and the natural world instead of having their basis in Christ. Only in Christ, Paul declares, does the fullness of God dwell, and only in Him will human beings ever be full and complete.

Trying to find satisfaction in any school of thought or belief system not rooted in the Word of God will always leave people empty and frustrated, and trying to add other philosophies to the Word of God will only lead to confusion. We need to be single-minded in our commitment to God's Word and to base all of our thoughts and belief systems on its truth. Jesus reigns over every philosophy and every way of thinking anyone could imagine. God has given Him all authority in heaven and on earth (Matthew 28:18), and He satisfies completely.

> ## Additional Reading
>
> **From *Do Yourself a Favor...Forgive***
>
> We cannot deal harshly and effectively with sin if we make excuses for it or keep it hidden. We should all examine our hearts and be bold enough to be honest with ourselves about any sinful behavior in our lives. The apostle Paul said that he worked diligently to maintain a conscience that was void of offense toward God and man (Acts 24:16). Wow! He worked at detecting and keeping sin out of his life. Paul knew the power of having a clean conscience before God. We should make every effort not to sin, but when we do, we should never make excuses for it or try to keep it hidden. Our secrets can make us miserable, but the truth makes us free.
>
> Romans 14:23 says that whatever is not of faith is sin. If we cannot do what we do in faith, then we should not do it. If something is sin, then call it sin—don't call it your problem, your hang-up, or your addiction. Sin is ugly, and if we cloak it in better-sounding words, we are more likely to keep it.
>
> We should examine our life in the light of God's Word, and anything that does not agree with it should be seen for what it is and resisted with all our God-given ability. If we ask Him, God will always help us. We are partners with God, and He never expects

us to do anything without His help. Let me say this one more time: Don't hide sin—bring it into the open, call it what it is, and don't make excuses for it or blame your bad choices on anyone else. Receive God's complete forgiveness for past sins, and work with the Holy Spirit to aggressively resist all temptation in the future.

Now, do yourself a favor and forgive yourself totally and completely. Give up any anger you might have toward yourself for perceived failures, and start living the good life God has prearranged and made ready for you to live (Ephesians 2:10).

## Think About It

What common ideas in today's culture conflict with God's Word, and how can you guard your heart against them?

_____

_____

_____

How does trusting in Christ guard us from the philosophies of the world?

_____

_____

_____

## Supporting Scripture

*For no one can lay any foundation other than the one already laid, which is Jesus Christ.*

1 Corinthians 3:11

## Put It to Work

Write down truths from God's Word that you can turn to when you encounter the world's temptations and philosophies. This week, when you notice those worldly ideas, reflect on these truths and ask the Holy Spirit for wisdom.

_____
_____
_____

## Your Personal Response

Take a good look at the influences in your life today—the people around you, what you see on social media, and the entertainment you consume. What worldly philosophies do you encounter that seem perfectly normal to others but contradict God's truth? List several that you notice.

For one of those worldly philosophies, find and write down a scripture that directly counters that lie. This will be your spiritual weapon the next time you encounter it.

Remember, we all face various influences daily. The difference lies in whether we recognize them and stand firm in God's truth or go along with the current tide of what everyone else thinks is normal.

_____
_____
_____
_____
_____
_____
_____

LESSON 7

# Pressing on Toward the Goal

## Let's Get Started

Write down several goals and dreams you have for your life. What are you doing to try to attain them?

_____
_____
_____

## Key Scripture Reading

*Not that I have already obtained all this, or have already arrived at my goal, but I press on to take hold of that for which Christ Jesus took hold of me. Brothers and sisters, I do not consider myself yet to have taken hold of it. But one thing I do: Forgetting what is behind and straining toward what is ahead, I press on toward the goal to win the prize for which God has called me heavenward in Christ Jesus.*

Philippians 3:12–14

## Dig Deeper

What are some of the distractions that make it hard for you to stay focused on "what is ahead"?

## Core Truth

Paul wants to make clear to his readers that he does not consider himself to have arrived at the fullness of all of his spiritual goals. He desires to be perfect, but he admits he has not reached that place. While it is often good to share our victories with others, it is also good to share our journeys. Paul was on his way to reaching his goals but readily admitted that he had not attained them. Our victory stories come after our journeys are complete, but to share only our victories without being honest about the challenges, difficulties, and pain of the journey never really helps people who are hurting. In fact, it may confuse them and make them wonder why others always seem to be enjoying victory while they are still in a difficult place with painful circumstances.

If we fear being vulnerable, we will often pretend everything is wonderful when, in reality, we are struggling and hurting. Paul didn't do that. He shared many victories but did not exclude his weaknesses and struggles from his writing.

If you were asked what the most important day in your life has been, what would you say? Some might say it was the day they married, graduated from college, or had their first child. While all of those are wonderful occasions, none of those answers would be correct, because the most important day of any of our lives is today! Many important days hold memories we cherish, but nothing compares to today—it matters more than you may realize.

Paul states that his one aspiration (hope, wish, desire) was to let go of those things that were behind and press toward the full will of God. Paul knew he could not make progress today if he held on to yesterday's mistakes. This is a very powerful truth that is important for us to realize. Today holds possibilities for those who embrace it and look earnestly for what it may hold for them. Today is important because once it is gone, you can never get it back again. Don't waste it worrying about the mistakes of the past.

I struggled with guilt and condemnation in a major way for close to fifty years. Having been abused sexually by my father and growing up in a home that was a mixture of my father's violence and abuse and my mother's fear and timidity, I did not have many opportunities to feel good about myself. I always assumed that something was wrong with me for my father to want to treat me in the despicable way he did. I had a recording that was on a loop playing over and over in my mind that said, "What's wrong with me? What's wrong with me?"

I have learned that carrying a burden of guilt leaves us weary, worn out, and exhausted—spiritually, mentally, emotionally, and physically. We were not built for guilt! God created us in His own image with a desire for us to love Him, love others, and love ourselves. He also wants us to love and fully enjoy our lives. But we cannot do that if we are stuck in our past mistakes, hurts, and injustices. Scripture instructs us to repent of our sins, to forgive those who hurt and wound us, and to totally let go of things from the past.

I carried a burden of guilt for many years, but even worse than guilt, I had shame—shame that was toxic. It was poison to my soul. I was not merely ashamed of what had been done to me, but at the very core of my being I was ashamed of myself because it had happened. I assumed that somehow it was my fault. Then I saw in Scripture that instead of shame, God would give me a double portion of all that had been stolen from me (Isaiah 61:7). Isaiah also prophesied that we would be delivered from the shame of our youth (Isaiah 54:4). I took these promises as my own, and although the journey was not easy, victory did come in due time.

If we do not let go of the past, we will miss the new things that God is doing in our lives. God is ready to help us anytime we need help, but we cannot hold on to old things and take hold of new things at the same time.

### Additional Reading

**From *A Leader in the Making***

We have got to learn to enjoy what we do. Whatever your job is, enjoy it. Don't spend your life waiting for things to change before you can get happy. Learn to be happy now.

Don't go around talking about how you feel all the time. Learn to make some decisions. Do some things on purpose. Go ahead and make the devil mad by being happy even though you may not feel like it. That will really drive him crazy.

In John 15, Jesus talks about abiding in Him. And abiding in Christ means staying in a place of rest. In verse 11 of that chapter He says, "I have told you these things, that My joy and delight may be in you, and that your joy and gladness may be of full measure and complete and overflowing" (AMPC).

It sounds to me like Jesus wants us to be happy. He says it here, and He also said it in John 10:10. In John 17:13, He prayed to the Father about His disciples, saying, "And now I am coming to You; I say these things while I am still in the world, so that My joy may be made full and complete and perfect in them [that they may experience My delight fulfilled in them, that My enjoyment may be perfected in their own souls, that they may have My gladness within them, filling their hearts]" (AMPC).

Jesus wants us to be glad. He wants us to have a merry heart. He wants us to put a smile on our face so everybody around us can feel happy and secure. But sometimes we are too selfish to care about how others feel. Yet we go to church and pat each other on the back and say, "I love you with the love of the Lord."

Our love life is seen in the little things we do for one another—or don't do because we don't feel like it. What a difference we could make in our household, in the church, in the world if we would start being a little more pleasant, just smile at each other, and have a merry heart. Our decision to be joyful is not only for our own happiness—it helps us move forward in faith, grow in love for others, and embrace the life God has for us.

## Think About It

Describe a past trauma or experience that made it hard to see what God was doing in your life.

_____

_____

Which of God's promises encourage you to look ahead to the hope of Jesus?

_____

_____

## Supporting Scripture

*Forget the former things; do not dwell on the past. See, I am doing a new thing! Now it springs up; do you not perceive it?*

Isaiah 43:18–19

## Put It to Work

Write down one practical step you can take to let go of something you're holding on to. Do you need to forgive someone, ask for forgiveness, or forgive yourself? If you're unsure, write a short prayer asking God to guide and encourage you as you take this step.

_____
_____
_____

## Your Personal Response

One of the hardest things about being human is the constant temptation to look in the rearview mirror at our crashes, failures, and wrong turns. God says, "Look ahead!" yet we keep looking back.

What is something from your past that you've held on to far too long—something that steals your joy today because you keep replaying it in your mind?

Write out Isaiah 43:18–19: "Forget the former things; do not dwell on the past. See, I am doing a new thing!" Take a few moments to meditate on this verse and reflect deeply.

Next, write about what God might be doing in your life right now—something you could be missing because you're too focused on yesterday.

Finish your time by saying, "I trust You, God. I trust You to do a new thing!"

_____
_____
_____
_____
_____
_____
_____

LESSON 8

# Knowing Jesus on a Deeper Level

## Let's Get Started

Who in your life knows you best? What has helped that relationship grow stronger?

_____
_____
_____

## Key Scripture Reading

*I want to know Christ—yes, to know the power of his resurrection and participation in his sufferings, becoming like him in his death, and so, somehow, attaining to the resurrection from the dead.*

Philippians 3:10–11

## Dig Deeper

In light of this verse, what does it mean to you to know Christ deeply?

_____
_____
_____

## Core Truth

I am partial to the Amplified Bible, Classic Edition rendering of Philippians 3:10, because it has helped me understand what Paul meant when he said he wanted to know Christ and the power of His resurrection:

> [For my determined purpose is] that I may know Him [that I may progressively become more deeply and intimately acquainted with Him, perceiving and recognizing and understanding the wonders of His Person more strongly and more clearly], and that I may in that same way come to know the power outflowing from His resurrection [which it exerts over believers], and that I may so share His sufferings as to be continually transformed [in spirit into His likeness even] to His death.

Let me ask you to stop and feel the depth of the cry of Paul's heart in this passage. He wasn't satisfied with merely knowing about Jesus or even just knowing Him a little; he wanted to know Him deeply and intimately. That goal, in fact, was his determined purpose. Many people know about Jesus or believe that He exists, but a much richer quality of life with Him is available to us. What fuels intimacy with God is time and including Him in every area of our lives.

Spending time with people and seeing them in all kinds of situations is the only way to truly know them. Our family is very close, and although my children are all adults who have their own families, they still call their mom and tell me what they are doing, or they share their joys or heartaches with Dave and me. You can love all your children the same yet feel closer to the ones who include you in their lives and also do things for you.

I believe the same principle applies to our relationship with God. It seems that the apostle John had a special, very intimate relationship with Jesus. He referred to himself as the disciple whom Jesus loved (John 13:23; 19:26). That might sound a bit haughty on his part, but it wasn't. John simply loved Jesus and had a real revelation of how much Jesus loved him. His goal, like Paul's, was intimacy with Jesus. I think anyone can be as close to God as they want to be. The level of intimacy a person enjoys with Him depends simply on how much time they are willing to put into building the relationship.

The time I am talking about is not an hour spent sitting in a church once a week. It is about including God in all we do. He is never more than one thought away from us, so I encourage you to think of Him often, whisper your gratitude to Him for different things all throughout the day, and ask for His help in everything, even in seemingly insignificant things. I ask the Lord to help me before I put in my contact lenses, before I work out, and before I approach any project, no matter how small. I am sorry for the times I have an independent attitude and spend the day doing many things without even asking for His help. You might say, "Well, Joyce, you got the things done anyway, so what difference does it make if you didn't ask for God's help?" I may have gotten the things done, but how much more joyfully, easily, and perhaps more quickly could I have accomplished them with God's help?

I certainly have not perfected this spiritual discipline. There have been plenty of times when I've gone about my busy schedule and suddenly the day was over, and I realized I hadn't thought of the Lord all day. I'm not suggesting that God will never help us unless we ask for His help in each specific task we undertake. But I believe we honor Him when we do, and doing so is a way to keep Him in our thoughts. I am hoping to establish the importance of always having the realization of how much we need the

Holy Spirit's help in all we do. This is not a law we must follow but a privilege we have, so why not take advantage of it?

## Additional Reading

**From *A Leader in the Making***

At the age of thirty-two, I found myself very frustrated because my Christianity didn't seem to be helping me in my practical, everyday life. I believed I would go to heaven when I died, but I was desperate for some help to get through each day on earth with peace and joy. My soul was filled with pain from the abuse of my childhood, and I manifested that pain daily in my attitudes and inability to maintain good relationships.

God's Word tells us that if we seek Him diligently, we will find Him (Proverbs 8:17). I began seeking God on my own for whatever I was missing, and I had an encounter with Him that brought me much closer to Him. He suddenly seemed very present in my daily life, and I began to study diligently in order to know Him better. It seemed that everywhere I turned, I heard about faith. I learned that I could apply my faith in many circumstances, which would open a door for God to get involved and help me.

I believed with all my heart that the principles I was learning were correct, but I still experienced great frustration because I couldn't seem to get them to work for me—at least not to the degree I desperately needed. At that time, God was using me in ministry; it was growing. I had definitely made tremendous progress, but I still felt deep within my heart that something was missing, so I once

# Knowing Jesus on a Deeper Level

> again began to seek God in a serious way. Through my searching and deeper study, I learned that I was missing the main lesson Jesus came to teach us: to love God, love others, and love ourselves (Matthew 22:36–39). I had learned a lot about faith as I walked with God, but I had not learned about the power of love.

## Think About It

What experiences or practices have most helped you grow in your relationship with Jesus?

_____
_____
_____
_____

What distractions or habits could you set aside to spend more meaningful time with Jesus?

_____
_____
_____
_____

## Supporting Scripture

*I no longer call you servants, because a servant does not know his master's business. Instead, I have called you friends, for everything that I learned from my Father I have made known to you. You did not choose me, but I chose you and appointed you so that you might go and bear fruit—fruit that will last—and so that whatever you ask in my name the Father will give you. This is my command: Love each other.*

John 15:15–17

## Put It to Work

What are some things you could do this week that would allow you to spend more time with Jesus? What distractions do you need to remove to be able to talk with Him and read His Word more?

_____
_____
_____

## Your Personal Response

On a scale of one to ten, how hungry are you to know Jesus more intimately? Don't just give the right answer—think about the real answer.

Next, on a scale of one to ten, where would you place yourself when it comes to including Jesus in everything you do?

Spend some time reflecting on what specific things need to change for you to move up on both of these scales.

Remember, knowing Jesus isn't about religious activity. It's not about checking boxes or looking good at church. It's about spending time in a relationship with Him. The more time you spend getting to know Him, the deeper your relationship will be.

_____
_____
_____

Knowing Jesus on a Deeper Level

## LOOKING BACK

What habits or choices can you begin today that will help you grow steadily and become more like Christ?

_____
_____
_____
_____
_____
_____
_____
_____

What lies do you still find yourself believing, even though they don't line up with God's Word?

_____
_____
_____
_____
_____
_____
_____
_____

How can you go deeper in your knowledge and understanding of Scripture, so that God's Word might dwell in you richly?

___

What are you holding on to that God is inviting you to release so you can move forward?

___

What kinds of things do you tend to ask God for, and how can you start asking for more of Him instead?

___

Looking Back

How can you let the light of Jesus shine through you more brightly in your workplace, friendships, or family?

# NOTES

Unless otherwise stated, scripture quotations are taken from the Holy Bible, New International Version®, NIV®. Copyright © 1973, 1978, 1984, 2011 by Biblica, Inc.™ Used by permission of Zondervan. All rights reserved worldwide. www.zondervan.com. The "NIV" and "New International Version" are trademarks registered in the United States Patent and Trademark Office by Biblica, Inc.™

Scripture quotations marked AMP are taken from the Amplified Bible, Copyright © 2015 by The Lockman Foundation. Used by permission. www.Lockman.org

Scripture quotations marked AMPC are taken from the Amplified Bible, Classic Edition, Copyright © 1954, 1958, 1962, 1964, 1965, 1987 by The Lockman Foundation. Used by permission. www.Lockman.org

Scripture quotations marked NKJV are taken from the New King James Version®. Copyright © 1982 by Thomas Nelson. Used by permission. All rights reserved.

*A Leader in the Making: Essentials to Being a Good Leader After God's Own Heart*, copyright © 2002 by Joyce Meyer.

*The Love Revolution*, copyright © 2009 by Joyce Meyer.

*Approval Addiction: Overcoming Your Need to Please Everyone*, copyright © 2005 by Joyce Meyer.

## Notes

*In Pursuit of Peace: 21 Ways to Conquer Anxiety, Fear, and Discontentment*, copyright © 2004 by Joyce Meyer.

*Habits of a Godly Woman*, copyright © 2020 by Joyce Meyer.

*Do Yourself a Favor…Forgive: Learn How to Take Control of Your Life Through Forgiveness*, copyright © 2012 by Joyce Meyer.

## *Do you have a real relationship with Jesus?*

God loves you! He created you to be a special, unique, one-of-a-kind individual, and He has a specific purpose and plan for your life. And through a personal relationship with your Creator—God—you can discover a way of life that will truly satisfy your soul.

No matter who you are, what you've done, or where you are in your life right now, God's love and grace are greater than your sin—your mistakes. Jesus willingly gave His life so you can receive forgiveness from God and have new life in Him. He's just waiting for you to invite Him to be your Savior and Lord.

If you are ready to commit your life to Jesus and follow Him, all you have to do is ask Him to forgive your sins and give you a fresh start in the life you are meant to live. Begin by praying this prayer...

*Lord Jesus, thank You for giving Your life for me and forgiving me of my sins so I can have a personal relationship with You. I am sincerely sorry for the mistakes I've made, and I know I need You to help me live right.*

*Your Word says in Romans 10:9, "If you declare with your mouth, 'Jesus is Lord,' and believe in your heart that God raised him from the dead, you will be saved" (NIV). I believe You are the Son of God and confess You as my Savior and Lord. Take me just as I am, and work in my heart, making me the person You want me to be. I want to live for You, Jesus, and I am so grateful that You are giving me a fresh start in my new life with You today.*

*I love You, Jesus!*

It's so amazing to know that God loves us so much! He wants to have a deep, intimate relationship with us that grows every day as we spend time with Him in prayer and Bible study. And we want to encourage you in your new life in Christ.

Please visit joycemeyer.org/KnowJesus to request Joyce's book *A New Way of Living*, which is our gift to you. We also have other free resources online to help you make progress in pursuing everything God has for you.

Congratulations on your fresh start in your life in Christ! We hope to hear from you soon.

## ABOUT THE AUTHOR

Joyce Meyer is one of the world's leading practical Bible teachers and a *New York Times* bestselling author. Joyce's books have helped millions of people find hope and restoration through Jesus Christ. Joyce's program, *Enjoying Everyday Life*, is broadcast on television and radio and online to millions worldwide in over 110 languages.

Through Joyce Meyer Ministries, Joyce teaches internationally on a number of topics with a particular focus on how the Word of God applies to our everyday lives. Her candid communication style allows her to share openly and practically about her experiences so others can apply what she has learned to their lives.

Joyce has authored more than 150 books, which have been translated into more than 164 languages, and over 39 million of her books have been distributed worldwide. Bestsellers include *Power Thoughts*; *The Confident Woman*; *Look Great, Feel Great*; *Starting Your Day Right*; *Ending Your Day Right*; *Approval Addiction*; *How to Hear from God*; *Beauty for Ashes*; and *Battlefield of the Mind*.

Joyce's passion to help people who are hurting is foundational to the vision of Hand of Hope, the missions arm of Joyce Meyer Ministries. Each year Hand of Hope provides millions of meals for the hungry and malnourished, installs freshwater wells in poor and remote areas, provides

## About the Author

critical relief after natural disasters, and offers free medical and dental care to thousands through their hospitals and clinics worldwide. Through Project GRL, women and children are rescued from human trafficking and provided safe places to receive an education, nutritious meals, and the love of God.

# JOYCE MEYER MINISTRIES

U.S. & FOREIGN OFFICE
ADDRESSES

**Joyce Meyer Ministries**
P.O. Box 655
Fenton, MO 63026
USA
(636) 349-0303

**Joyce Meyer Ministries—Canada**
P.O. Box 7700
Vancouver, BC V6B 4E2
Canada
(800) 868-1002

**Joyce Meyer Ministries—Australia**
Locked Bag 77
Mansfield Delivery Centre
Queensland 4122
Australia
(07) 3349 1200

**Joyce Meyer Ministries—England**
P.O. Box 1549
Windsor SL4 1GT
United Kingdom
01753 831102

**Joyce Meyer Ministries—South Africa**
P.O. Box 5
Cape Town 8000
South Africa
(27) 21-701-1056

**Joyce Meyer Ministries—Francophonie**
29 avenue Maurice Chevalier
77330 Ozoir la Ferriere
France

**Joyce Meyer Ministries—Germany**
Postfach 761001
22060 Hamburg
Germany
+49 (0)40 / 88 88 4 11 11

**Joyce Meyer Ministries—Netherlands**
Lorenzlaan 14
7002 HB Doetinchem
+31 657 555 9789

**Joyce Meyer Ministries—Russia**
P.O. Box 789
Moscow 101000
Russia
+7 (495) 727-14-68

## OTHER BOOKS BY JOYCE MEYER

*100 Inspirational Quotes*
*100 Ways to Simplify Your Life*
*21 Ways to Finding Peace and Happiness*
*The Answer to Anxiety*
*Any Minute*
*Approval Addiction*
*The Approval Fix*
*Authentically, Uniquely You**
*The Battle Belongs to the Lord*
*Battlefield of the Mind**
*Battlefield of the Mind Bible*
*Battlefield of the Mind for Kids*
*Battlefield of the Mind for Teens*
*Battlefield of the Mind Devotional*
*Battlefield of the Mind New Testament*
*Be Anxious for Nothing**
*Be Joyful*
*Beauty for Ashes*
*Beginning Your Day God's Way*
*Being the Person God Made You to Be*
*Blessed in the Mess**
*Change Your Words, Change Your Life*
*Colossians: A Biblical Study*
*The Confident Mom*
*The Confident Woman*
*The Confident Woman Devotional*
*The Courage to Change*
*Do It Afraid**
*Do Yourself a Favor...Forgive*
*Eat the Cookie...Buy the Shoes*
*Eight Ways to Keep the Devil Under Your Feet*
*Ending Your Day Right*
*Enjoying Where You Are on the Way to Where You Are Going*
*Ephesians: A Biblical Study*
*The Everyday Life Bible*
*The Everyday Life Psalms and Proverbs*
*Filled with the Spirit*
*Finding God's Will for Your Life*
*Galatians: A Biblical Study*

*Good Health, Good Life*
*Habits of a Godly Woman*
*Healing the Soul of a Woman**
*Healing the Soul of a Woman Devotional*
*Healing the Wounds of Rejection*
*Hearing from God Each Morning*
*How to Age Without Getting Old*
*How to Hear from God **
*How to Succeed at Being Yourself*
*How to Talk with God*
*I Dare You*
*If Not for the Grace of God**
*In Pursuit of Peace*
*In Search of Wisdom*
*James: A Biblical Study*
*The Joy of an Uncluttered Life*
*The Joy of Believing Prayer*
*The Keys to a Happy and Healthy Marriage*
*Knowing God Intimately*
*A Leader in the Making*
*Life in the Word*
*Living Beyond Your Feelings*
*Living Courageously*
*Look Great, Feel Great*
*Love Out Loud*
*The Love Revolution*
*Loving People Who Are Hard to Love*
*Making Good Habits, Breaking Bad Habits*
*Making Marriage Work* (previously published as *Help Me—I'm Married!*)
*Managing Your Emotions*
*Me and My Big Mouth!**
*The Mind Connection**
*Mornings with God*
*My Time with God*
*Never Give Up!*
*Never Lose Heart*
*New Day, New You*
*Overcoming Every Problem*
*Overload*
*The Pathway to Success*
*The Penny*
*Perfect Love* (previously published as *God Is Not Mad at You*)*

*Philippians: A Biblical Study*
*The Power of Being Positive*
*The Power of Being Thankful*
*The Power of Determination*
*The Power of Forgiveness*
*The Power of Simple Prayer*
*Power Thoughts*
*Power Thoughts Devotional*
*Powerful Thinking*
*Quiet Times with God Devotional*
*Reduce Me to Love*
*The Secret Power of Speaking God's Word*
*The Secret to True Happiness*
*The Secrets of Spiritual Power*
*Seven Things That Steal Your Joy*
*Start Your New Life Today*
*Starting Your Day Right*
*Straight Talk*
*Teenagers Are People Too!*
*Trusting God Day by Day*
*Uniquely You*
*What About Me?\**
*The Word, the Name, the Blood*
*Woman to Woman*
*You Can Begin Again*
*Your Battles Belong to the Lord\**

## JOYCE MEYER SPANISH TITLES

*Amar a la gente que es muy difícil de amar (Loving People Who Are Hard to Love)*
*Auténtica y única (Authentically, Uniquely You)*
*Belleza en lugar de cenizas (Beauty for Ashes)*
*Benedicion en el desorden (Blessed in the Mess)*
*Buena salud, buena vida (Good Health, Good Life)*
*Cambia tus palabras, cambia tu vida (Change Your Words, Change Your Life)*
*El campo de batalla de la mente (Battlefield of the Mind)*
*Cómo envejecer sin avejentarse (How to Age Without Getting Old)*
*Como formar buenos habitos y romper malos habitos (Making Good Habits, Breaking Bad Habits)*
*La conexión de la mente (The Mind Connection)*
*Dios no está enojado contigo (God Is Not Mad at You)*
*La dosis de aprobación (The Approval Fix)*

*Efesios: Comentario bíblico (Ephesians: Biblical Commentary)*
*Empezando tu día bien (Starting Your Day Right)*
*Hágalo con miedo (Do It Afraid)*
*Hazte un favor a ti mismo...perdona (Do Yourself a Favor...Forgive)*
*Madre segura de sí misma (The Confident Mom)*
*Momentos de quietud con Dios (Quiet Times with God Devotional)*
*Mujer segura de sí misma (The Confident Woman)*
*No se afane por nada (Be Anxious for Nothing)*
*Pensamientos de poder (Power Thoughts)*
*Sanidad para el alma de una mujer (Healing the Soul of a Woman)*
*Sanidad para el alma de una mujer, devocionario (Healing the Soul of a Woman Devotional)*
*Santiago: Comentario bíblico (James: Biblical Commentary)*
*Sobrecarga (Overload)\**
*Sus batallas son del Señor (Your Battles Belong to the Lord)*
*Termina bien tu día (Ending Your Day Right)*
*Tienes que atreverte (I Dare You)*
*Usted puede comenzar de nuevo (You Can Begin Again)*
*Viva amando su vida (Living a Life You Love)*
*Viva valientemente (Living Courageously)*
*Vive por encima de tus sentimientos (Living Beyond Your Feelings)*
*Y que hay de mi (What About Me?)*

*\*Study Guide available for this title*

## BOOKS BY DAVE MEYER

*Life Lines*

"Now the Lord is the Spirit, and where the Spirit of the Lord is, there is freedom. And we all, who with unveiled faces contemplate the Lord's glory, are being transformed into his image with ever-increasing glory, which comes from the Lord, who is the Spirit."

2 Corinthians 3:17–18

---

"I want to know Christ—yes, to know the power of his resurrection and participation in his sufferings, becoming like him in his death, and so, somehow, attaining to the resurrection from the dead."

Philippians 3:10–11

---

"Do not conform to the pattern of this world, but be transformed by the renewing of your mind. Then you will be able to test and approve what God's will is—his good, pleasing and perfect will."

Romans 12:2

---

"Let the message of Christ dwell among you richly as you teach and admonish one another with all wisdom through psalms, hymns, and songs from the Spirit, singing to God with gratitude in your hearts."

Colossians 3:16

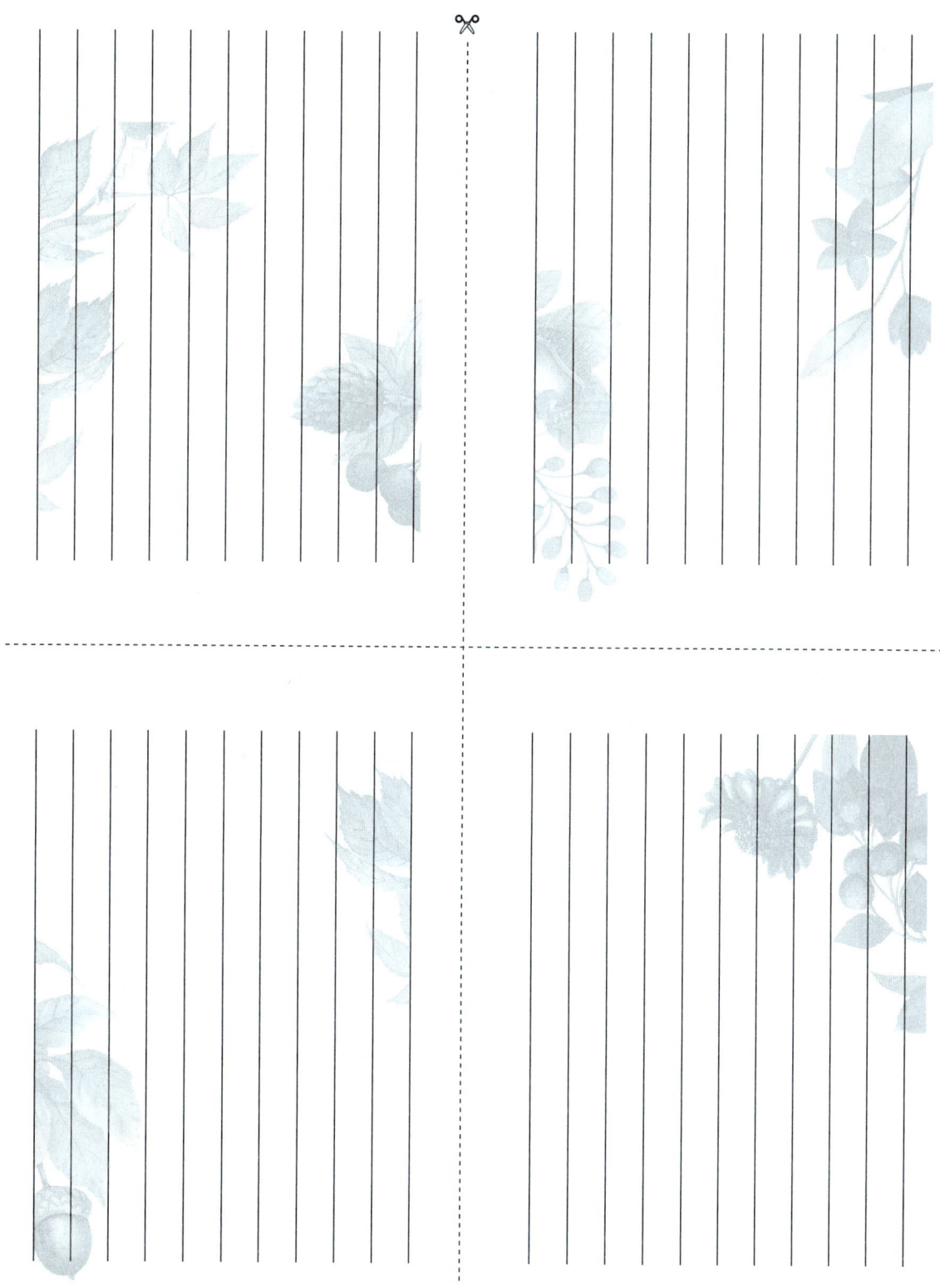

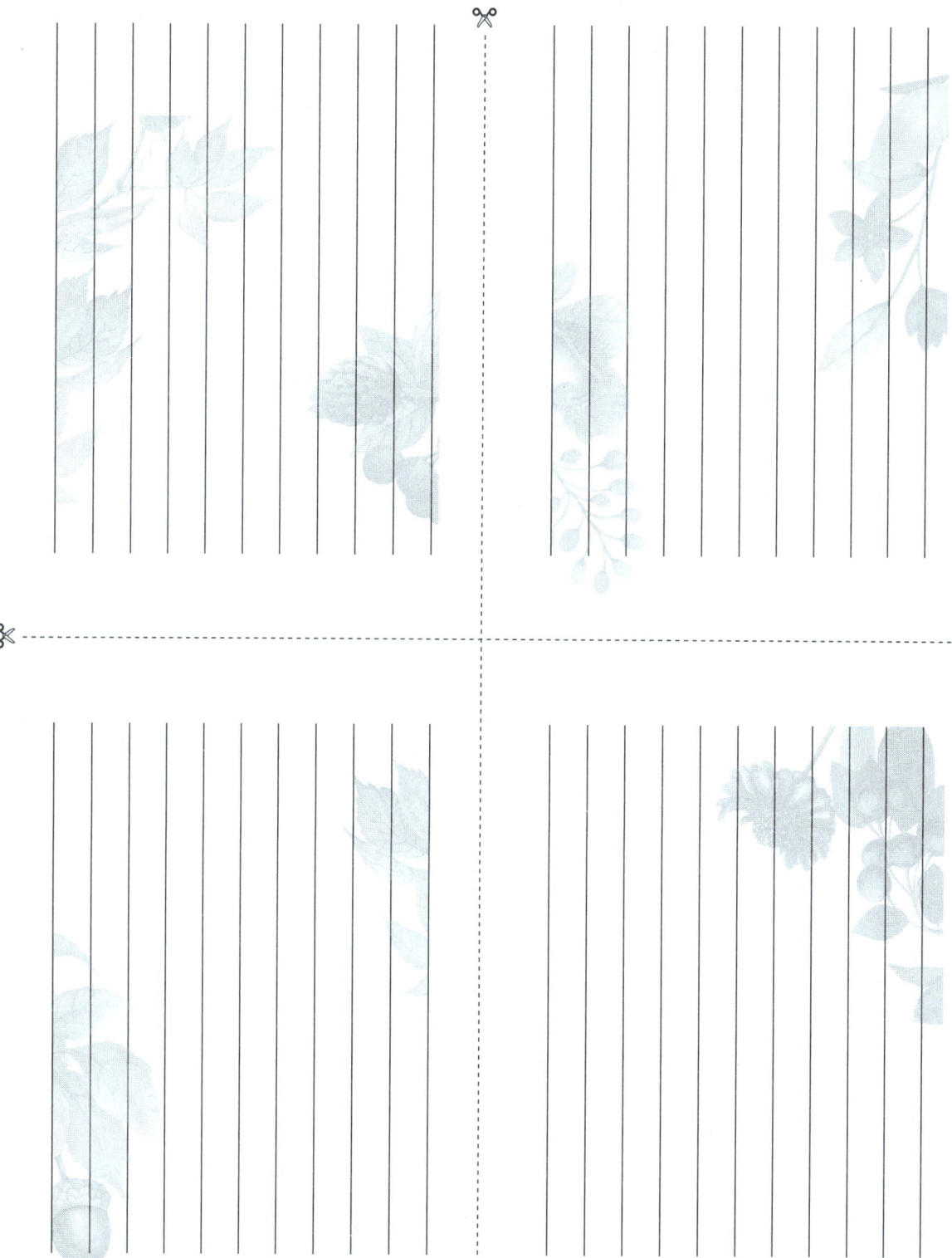

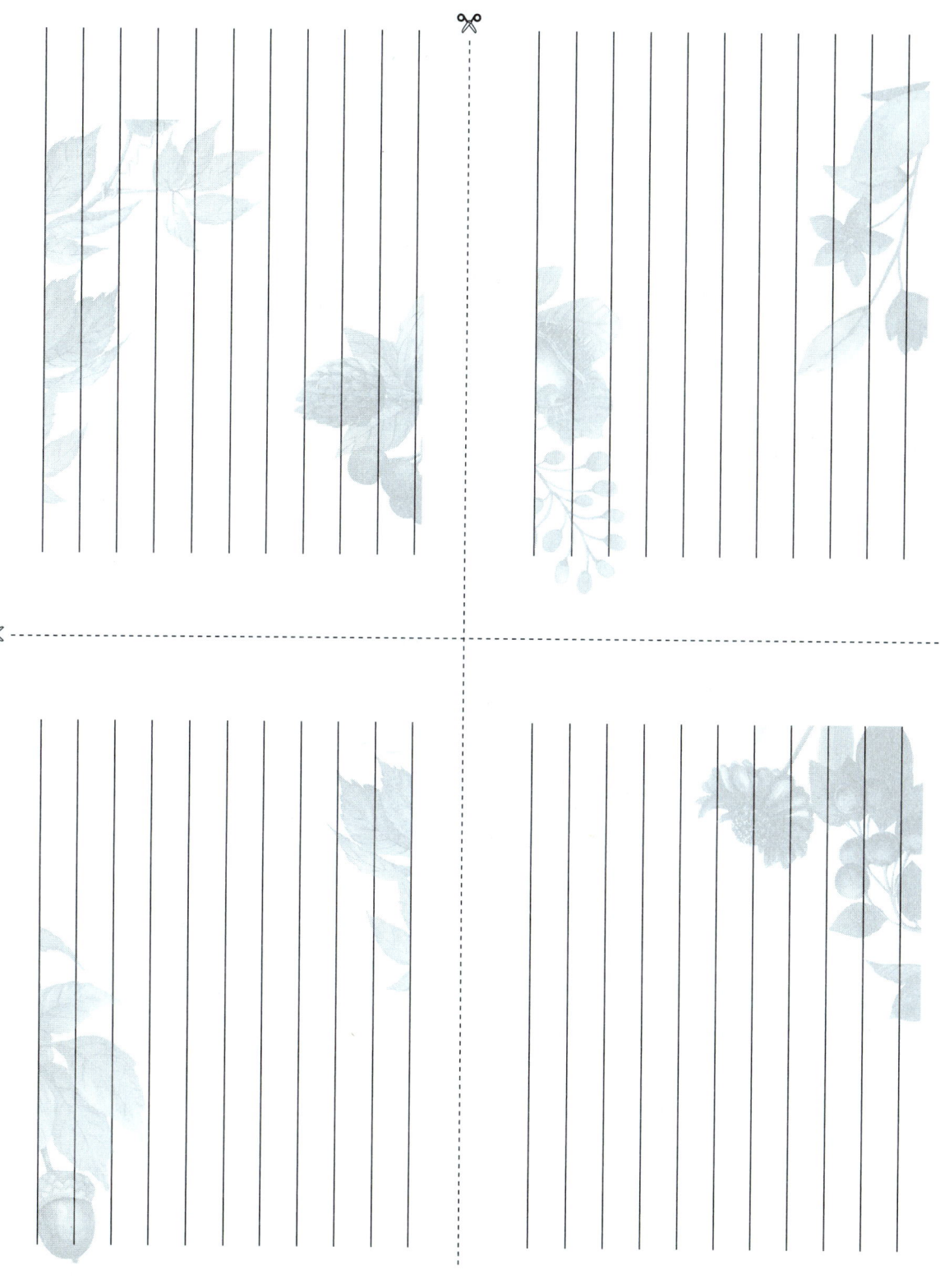